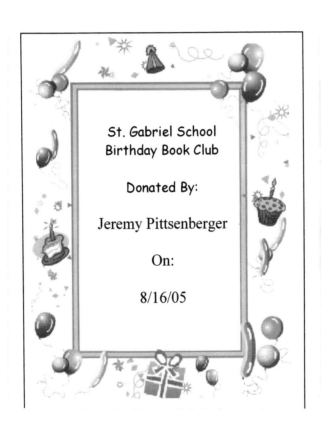

St. Gabriel School
Birthday Book Club

Donated By:

Jeremy Pittsenberger

On:

8/16/05

DREW
BLEDSOE

DREW BLEDSOE

COOL QUARTERBACK

Jeff Savage

Lerner Publications Company • Minneapolis

Library binding by Lerner Publications Company
241 First Avenue North, Minneapolis, Minnesota 55401

Website address: www.lernerbooks.com

Library of Congress Cataloging-in-Publication Data

Savage, Jeff, 1961–
    Drew Bledsoe, cool quarterback / Jeff Savage.
      p. cm.
    Includes bibliographical references (p.) and index.
    Summary: A biography of the New England Patriots quarterback who
led the team to the Superbowl in 1997.
    ISBN 0–8225–3670–6 (hardcover : alk. paper).
    1. Bledsoe, Drew, 1972–   —Juvenile literature. 2. Football
players—United States—Biography—Juvenile literature. 3. New
England Patriots (Football team)—Juvenile literature.
    [1. Bledsoe, Drew, 1972–   2. Foorball players.] I. Title.
GV939.B56S28   1999
796.332'092—dc21
    [b]   98–24212

Manufactured in the United States of America
1 2 3 4 5 6 – JR – 04 03 02 01 00 99

Contents

Drew drops back to pass in Super Bowl XXXI.

Cool in the Clutch

Drew Bledsoe walked off the field with the aching eyes of a boy who had just lost his puppy. He had thrown an interception on his fourth pass of the game. It was a simple down-and-out pass, but he had thrown it too softly and it hadn't reached his receiver. Drew's New England Patriots teammates left the field with him. Some were hanging their heads. Others stared up at the New Orleans Superdome roof and wondered if their quarterback was good enough for this game.

The Green Bay Packers were already ahead 7–0. They had scored on their second play with a 54-yard bomb from quarterback Brett Favre to wide receiver Andre Rison. As Drew took a seat on his team's bench, the Packers were ready to score again. Barely six minutes into the 1997 Super Bowl, the Packers kicked a field goal and the Patriots trailed 10–0.

During the pregame introductions, the Patriots had stormed onto the field in their slick white uniforms with red letters and blue trim. The New England players were determined to show that they were every bit as good as the Packers. But they knew it all depended on Drew. Even Packers coach Mike Holmgren had said so seconds before kickoff. He told a sideline reporter, **"Turnovers** will be a big part of this game. And, really, whichever quarterback plays the best today, that team is going to win."

Drew had responded before. The Patriots had started the season with two losses, but he rallied them to win 11 of their next 14 games. He had thrown for more than 4,000 yards and was an easy choice for the Pro Bowl. Nothing seemed to rattle him. He never got too happy. He never got too low. He always stayed steady and cool. "Win or lose," he said the day before the Super Bowl, "when I come home, my dogs will jump all over me." Reporters reminded him that this was the Super Bowl. The *Super Bowl.* Drew smiled and said, "Yes, it'll be on a huge stage, with however many billion people watching. But in a lot of ways, it feels like just another game."

Down by two scores and with the odds against him, Drew returned to the field and calmly called a play in the huddle. Beneath the calm face there was fire in his belly. Drew wanted to win. He *really* wanted to win. With a splendid mix of creative plays, he led his team down the field for a touchdown. First, he laid a perfect **screen pass** into the stomach of fullback Keith Byars. Byars cut upfield and broke several tackles for a 32-yard gain. Next, Drew whipped a sidearm pass around hulking Packers lineman Reggie White, into the hands of wide receiver Terry Glenn for a gain of 20 more. Finally, Drew feathered a pass over the top to wide receiver Shawn Jefferson, who had beaten his defender. Packers cornerback Craig Newsome prevented the score by grabbing Jefferson's face mask.

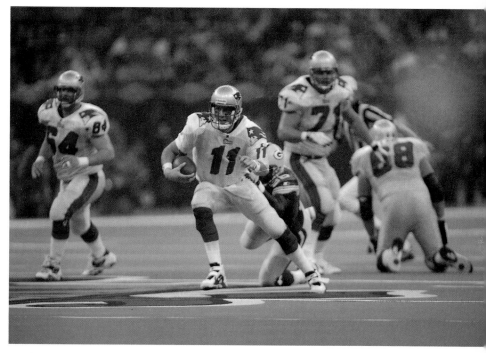

Scrambling in the Patriots' pocket, Drew looks for help.

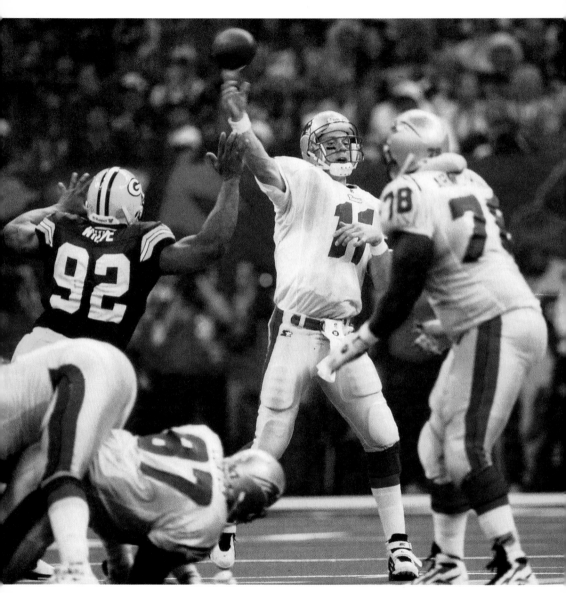

Drew's powerful arm is one of his strongest assets.

The penalty called on Newsome put the Patriots at the 1-yard line. On the next play, Drew faked a hand-off and whistled a ball to Byars in the end zone for the touchdown. The score became 10–7.

The Packers were forced to punt soon after they got the ball. Drew brought his offense back on the field for more. His first play was a nifty pass to running back Curtis Martin that was good for 7 yards to midfield. Next, Martin bashed ahead for 2 more yards. That set up a third-**down** situation with only a yard to go for another first down.

Martin started forward and Drew tucked the ball into the running back's arms. Martin lunged into the belly of the defense, where the Packers swallowed him up. But the play was a fake. Drew still had the ball. He was hunched over and cradling it 10 yards behind the line of scrimmage. Drew rose up to his full 6 feet 5 inches and looked downfield. The Packers were nowhere near him. He gave the ball his trademark pat with the left hand. Then with an effortless flick, he launched the ball. It arched high, spinning tightly through the Superdome air. Seventy-three thousand people in the stands breathlessly watched as it descended to Terry Glenn, who left his feet to catch it in a sprawl at the 4-yard line. A roar rang out as Patriots fans twirled a sea of blue pompons.

The brilliant play was a snatch of hocus-pocus that Drew had learned as a young boy in eastern

Washington. His father, Mac, was a high school coach and had taught him such tricks. Awestruck television analyst John Madden bellowed, "That's part of having a dad as a coach! He learned things like **play-fakes** and screens before he learned how to use a knife and fork!"

Drew finished the drive by rolling right and firing a strike to tight end Ben Coates in the end zone. "His ball will get up on you really fast," Coates once said. "He'll hit you in the face mask if you're not careful." Coates threw himself to the carpet and speared the pass for the touchdown. Drew raised his arms in triumph. Suddenly, the Patriots were hopping around the field like jumping beans. It was still the first quarter, but Drew had proved that he was cool in the clutch.

Across the field, the Packers were kicking the ground and yelling at one another. "We were completely baffled," safety LeRoy Butler said. "No one had pushed us around all year, and they were killing us, doing stuff we hadn't seen before." Defensive coordinator Fritz Shurmur gathered his squad together and screamed, "Enough is enough! Go do what you're supposed to do!" Then to Butler he said, "Go get Bledsoe. Do whatever it takes. I'll **blitz** you every play if I have to—just get in his face! I want him to worry about where you are all the time!"

On defense, the Packers started rushing five or six players at Drew at a time. The Patriots failed to adjust. Coach Bill Parcells did not keep enough players inside to block for his quarterback. With Drew getting blitzed from all angles, the next four New England drives fizzled. Meanwhile, Green Bay went on a scoring spree. Favre threw a record-breaking 81-yard touchdown bomb to Antonio Freeman. Chris Jacke kicked his second field goal. Favre scrambled two yards for another touchdown just before the half.

Mixing passes with runs, Drew prepares to hand off.

Green Bay's defenders made life miserable for Drew in the 1997 Super Bowl by blitzing on many plays.

New England trailed by two scores again, 27–14. The Patriots were desperate for a spark.

After just missing Jefferson with a long pass on the team's first drive of the third quarter, Drew started the Patriots again at their own 47-yard line. On third down with 5 yards to go for a first down, he fired a

14

pass that was so hard it hit Coates in the chest and bounced off. Luckily, the big tight end grabbed it out of the air and held on for a 13-yard gain. Then Drew completed a pass to Jefferson for 9 more. With the Patriots at the 18-yard line, the Packers expected another pass. Drew crossed them up by handing off to Martin, who burst up the middle to the end zone. Suddenly it was 27–21.

The Patriots could win this game! In Drew's first four seasons, he had thrown for 14,642 yards and 80 touchdowns. No quarterback in NFL history had accomplished so much before his 25th birthday. If Drew and the Patriots could beat the Packers, he would be the youngest quarterback ever to win the Super Bowl. Joe Montana and Joe Namath had both been 25 years and 227 days old when they won it. Drew was just 24.

The Patriots' hopes came crashing down on the very next play. After the Patriots kicked off, Desmond Howard raced up the middle with the ball. He ran, untouched, 99 yards for a Green Bay touchdown. Drew watched helplessly as the team in green and gold rollicked with joy across the field. The Packers added a two-point **conversion** to make the score 35–21. The Packers knew that the Patriots had to throw on nearly every play to have a chance. The Green Bay defense kept a relentless rush swarming all around Drew. Neither team scored again.

After sacking Drew again, the Packers defenders celebrate.

Drew sat in the locker room after the game, his fore-head beaded with sweat and his hair matted. He wondered what more he could have done to help his team win. "For us to win the game," he told reporters, "I knew I had to play at a very high level, and the team had to play at a very high level. Neither happened."

The Packers had played a nearly perfect game to win. They committed no turnovers and were called for only three penalties. Even so, they had still needed a record-breaking kickoff return to assure a Packer victory. Reporters asked Drew if this loss would shake his faith in himself. "I'm not going to let this game or any one game affect my confidence," he said. "Obviously, optimism is hard to come by when you've just lost the Super Bowl. But this is a good young team and we're going to commit to working hard this off-season." Then he excused himself, got dressed, and walked out of the stadium into the cool night.

Drew congratulates Green Bay quarterback Brett Favre.

Barbara and Mac Bledsoe celebrate Christmas with Drew.

2
Small-Town Childhood

Drew McQueen Bledsoe grew up in central and eastern Washington, the land of sweet onions and wheat. He was born on Valentine's Day in 1972 to Mac and Barbara Bledsoe. Mac and Barbara had met at Morgan Junior High School in Ellensburg, Washington. They became childhood sweethearts. "He was tall and handsome and wore white button-down shirts with blue jeans, and he was a good athlete," Barbara said. "He was a nice boy and he caught my eye." Mac went away to play football at the University of Washington, then returned to Ellensburg. He and Barbara became schoolteachers and started a family. Mac also coached the football team.

Drew was surrounded by a close and loving family. Grandpa Stu was a rancher who had once served as the state speaker of the house. He often thrilled Drew with stories of his days as a fighter pilot in World War II.

19

Drew loved playing with his Grandma Maxine and
Grandpa Dick on their farm in Washington.

Grandma Betsy liked to take Drew and his brother
Adam, who was six years younger, to the state capitol
building or out to restaurants to teach them proper
manners. Grandpa Dick often left his farming chores to
come into the house and sit at the living room window
with young Drew on his lap. Together they would read
or just stare at trees. Grandma Maxine taught Drew to
appreciate flowers, and she often took Drew down to
Menastash Creek to skip stones on the water.

Drew's first childhood friend was Kristi Klump,
who lived across the street from the Bledsoe home in
Ellensburg. Kristi was a year older than Drew. She
taught Drew how to play with dolls. He showed her
how to be rough-and-tumble and ride tricycles.

20

Drew was just a year old when his father began taking him to the All-Northwest Football Camp. Mac helped run the summer football camp, which featured NFL players as guest instructors. Oakland Raiders star Fred Biletnikoff was there Drew's first year. One afternoon, the All-Pro wide receiver took off an expensive pair of shoes before going swimming. Mac and Fred were talking when Mac glanced over Fred's shoulder. "I hope our friendship is strong, because it's about to be tested," Mac said. Biletnikoff asked what he meant. Mac pointed to one-year-old Drew and said, "That's my son over there and he's peeing in your shoes."

Drew's dad often read to Drew and his brother, Adam.

When Drew was four, his family moved from Ellensburg 90 miles north to Wenatchee so Mac could coach at the local junior college. A year later, they moved a bit farther up the road to Waterville, a quiet community of a few hundred people. Drew remembers that he had "the run of the town." In the winter, he sledded and skied. In the summer, he swam and ran through the wheat fields. He often played with Jed Barnes, whose father was a farmer. The two boys like to ride the combine—a big machine that cut and threshed grain in the field.

Once Drew and another friend were playing with matches in a vacant lot down the street from Drew's house. A whiff of wind came up and suddenly the field was ablaze. After firefighters put out the fire, Drew was put in the backseat of the sheriff's car, his wide eyes peeking out the window at his crying mother. Drew was taken to the police station. His punishment was to write a letter of apology. He had to write the letter to every firefighter and police officer in town. Then he had to stand before them at the firehouse and read it aloud.

Drew loved to go to his father's summer football camps each year. He said he learned football "the way a normal kid learns language. I've known cover-two and cover-three **(defensive formations)** since I was in the third grade." He paid attention to the NFL instructors, studying how they conducted themselves.

Drew liked all sorts of sports as a child, including track.

"The biggest realization I had from watching them was that they were real people," he said. "I realized that if you have talent for playing football, it doesn't make you any different from anybody else."

When Drew was in fourth grade, his family moved again, this time east to Benton City. He played sports in the neighborhood with his new friend, Scott Morris. Sometimes they came up with games of their own. Along with Adam, they liked to pin towels to their shoulders and run around like cartoon superheroes. Mac says his son's favorite subjects in elementary school were, in order, "recess, lunch, after-school games, and then everything else."

As a fourth grader, Drew loved playing games with friends in Benton City.

As active as Drew was, however, he could also be quiet and calm. He didn't mind spending hours at a time doing his homework. "When Adam was a baby and I was having a hard day with him," said Barbara, "Drew would say, 'Mom, let me take care of him. You go take it easy.' He'd pick Adam up, and they'd walk around and look at plants and things."

Drew admired the football players at his father's practices at Kiona-Benton High School, but especially Ricky Dunn, the quarterback. Ricky had a motorcycle. Drew wanted to be like Ricky, so Drew asked his parents if he could buy a small off-road motorcycle. He had saved the money he'd gotten for his birthday, plus the allowance he earned by doing household chores like mowing the lawn. "He didn't mow the lawn cheerfully," said his mother. "You could see him muttering to himself as he mowed." Drew's parents told him all the reasons he should not be allowed to own a motorcycle. Mac concluded by saying that it

24

was a big responsibility. "But Dad," Drew said, "I *am* responsible." There was no argument about that. Soon Drew was riding his new yellow dirt bike.

When Drew was in the sixth grade, his family moved to Walla Walla, in the valley of the Blue Mountains. There they rented a ranch house on Hood Place, out by the airport. Later they bought a home on Russell Creek Road. Drew and Adam rode their dirt bikes through the rolling wheat fields, and Mac said, "Drew was always crowding the speed limit."

Drew gives a friend a ride on his brand new dirt bike.

Drew became fast friends with Gus Rojas, Brent Partlow, Cary Flanagan, and Andy Jamison. Together they water-skied, jumped their bikes, and played football.

Drew wanted to be a quarterback, but as a seventh grader at Pioneer Junior High School, he was beaten out by a boy named Tommy Knecht. Knecht was a good athlete who later played linebacker at Stanford University. Drew's junior high coach, Dave Klicker, told Drew to choose another position to play. "Coach Klicker said I shouldn't play quarterback," Drew told his father that evening at home. "He said I'm not fast enough, I don't throw that far, and my throws aren't accurate enough." Mac looked at his son and said, "Well, it sounds like you know the things you need to work on." Then he told Drew that he should never allow someone else to rule his dreams.

For the next two years, Drew played tight end. But after practice each day and on weekends, he threw hundreds of passes to Andy Jamison. Drew was determined to be a quarterback. Before his ninth-grade year at Pioneer, Tommy Knecht moved away. Drew became the 49ers quarterback. He was 6 feet 3 inches tall and weighed just 125 pounds. His father said he looked like a praying mantis. But with his strong arm, Drew was able to throw a pass far downfield.

Drew regularly went to his father's practices at Walla Walla High, just to be around his high school heroes.

Once when the senior quarterback failed to understand a new play, Drew's father asked him to show the players how to run it. Drew executed the play perfectly and completed the pass. At that moment, he realized he could be a high school quarterback. "By about eighth grade, Drew had a picture of where he was going," Mac said. "If he'd lived up to my expectations, he'd have been a tight end at Montana. But he knew exactly what he wanted to do."

For a ninth-grade graduation gift, Drew's parents gave him a ski trip with his pal Jed Barnes. The two boys flew to Los Angeles, California, then switched planes and headed to Utah for three days of skiing. Drew realized his parents trusted him to make good decisions. He felt proud, confident, and loved.

Drew, fourth from the right, stands next to his friend, Andy Jamison (No. 11), as the Walla Walla High School seniors are recognized during a home game.

28

Emerging Dreams

3

Friday nights in Walla Walla were like Friday nights everywhere in America. High school athletes played football beneath the lights and the townsfolk came out with their blankets and seat cushions to watch. The Walla Walla High Blue Devils played their games at Borleske Stadium, an old building along the Union Pacific railroad tracks and Highway 12. Truckers on the highway honked their horns as they passed.

When Drew entered Walla Walla High, the football team had senior Joe Volek at quarterback and junior Jason Linke as a backup. Drew was given jersey number 12 and assigned to the junior varsity. Drew proved himself and played well on the junior varsity, but the varsity team struggled to move the ball. Four games into the season, the assistant coaches pleaded with Mac and his co-head coach to let Drew play for the varsity. Reluctantly, they agreed. "It was a tough spot," said Mac. "I didn't want Drew getting any favoritism, or any players thinking he was getting any. I didn't want any hurt feelings." Instead, in his first varsity game, Drew got hurt. A lineman for the powerful Borah High team from Boise, Idaho, slammed Drew in the stomach with his helmet. The blow pushed Drew's liver into his backbone. Doctors found a softball-sized hematoma, a bruise filled with blood, on Drew's liver.

Drew had to avoid any contact for many weeks to allow the swelling to go down. As he recovered and regained his strength, Drew was trying to figure out a few things. For one, he decided not to drink alcohol. He thought that to be a great athlete he needed to take care of his body. He told his parents, "You only have to make the decision once. It's not a decision you have to make every weekend." Drew's friends accepted his choice, but he wasn't always invited to parties. There were times when he was lonely. He found strength through his parents and the values they shared.

By the summer of his junior year, Drew had committed himself fully to becoming a great quarterback. He worked out at a YMCA, using old weight lifting machines that were too small for his body, which had filled out to 185 pounds. He threw passes to his pal Andy Jamison for hours a day at a nearby elementary school. When fall practice began, Drew's passes were crisp spirals, bullseye straight.

Drew, third from the right in the back row, was a member of the homecoming court at Walla Walla High School.

Drew had a new coach that fall. Gary Mires had moved from Oregon to be the head coach. Drew's dad was the offensive coach. "Drew could throw the football, that's for sure," said Coach Mires, "but really it was his determination that made him special."

When Drew's mother did his laundry, she would find notes he had written for himself in his pockets. They said things like *I hustle on every play* or *The team always comes first* or *I'm the first on the field and the last to leave.* "Nobody was supposed to see those notes," said Drew. "But moms find everything."

In a practice drill one day just before the season began, Andy Jamison broke his leg. The Blue Devils didn't have many wide receivers to begin with, and now Drew had lost his favorite target. The Blue

Devils had to persuade a basketball player, Ricky Wilson, to join the team as a receiver. Walla Walla lost its first game, won its second, and then beat Eisenhower High of Yakima, 31–9. In that game, Drew connected with Wilson 16 times for 265 yards.

Next the Blue Devils traveled to Boise to play mighty Borah. Drew didn't get hurt this time, but his team got pummeled, 54–6. Something good came of the trip, though. Weber State head coach Mike Price happened to be at the game. During the warmups, he was down on the field next to Coach Mires when he noticed Drew. "Man, that kid can really throw," Coach Price said. "He's really going to be a college prospect." Walla Walla won two more games to finish with a 4–5 record. That season, Drew led his conference with more than 1,600 yards passing.

By this time, Drew stood 6 feet 4 and he played basketball in the winter. But he could not crack the starting lineup on the basketball team, so he cheered for his buddies from his seat on the bench. In the spring, Drew was on the track team. He threw the javelin 190 feet and broke the school record in the high jump at 6 feet, 7 inches. Still, football was his love. "The best day in track," he said, "is not as good as the worst practice in football."

Drew's best day in football came late in the summer before his senior season. Mike Price had become the coach at Washington State University (WSU).

Although Drew (No. 43) was on the Walla Walla boys' basketball team, he didn't play much.

Coach Price and his staff came to Walla Walla to teach the coaches and players how to play WSU's style of offense. "It was sure nice of Coach Price to do that for us," said Coach Mires, "but I think he had an ulterior motive." Coach Price was hoping that

Drew finished high school with a 3.67 grade point average.

Drew would enjoy the passing plays and want to play for WSU. To everyone's delight, Drew excelled in the new system. In the season opener, he made what Coach Mires called "the greatest play I've ever seen." Drew was clobbered by a blitzing linebacker, yet he managed to stay on his feet and deliver a 45-yard strike between two defenders to Mike Gonzales for a touchdown. In another game, Drew broke the state record with 509 passing yards. During the season, he produced 2,560 yards and 25 touchdowns, leading the Blue Devils to a 6–3 record. "He never got emotional one way or another, never too excited and never too down," said Coach Mires. "He was so focused and cool. He was kind of your perfect kid."

College coaches from Stanford, Miami, and Washington wanted Drew to play for their teams. But Drew had a soft spot for Washington State in the college town of Pullman. "All they can do is offer me media exposure and a huge stadium," Drew said of the big-time colleges. "Neither of those things would make me very happy. I can go to Pullman and still play against those teams." The Cougars had been mediocre for years, managing as many as six wins just twice in 10 years. But the little town and the university that local people called "the Wazzu" fit Drew perfectly. "I kind of wanted to come to a place where the tradition wasn't so established," he said.

Drew could hardly wait to get to Pullman, but he kept focused on his studies because he wanted to finish high school with a flourish. He learned calculus. More than once his father had to tell him, "Just go to bed. Finish that school paper in the morning." He scored over 1,200 on the Scholastic Aptitude Test, finished high school with a grade point average of 3.67, and was chosen as a national merit scholarship honorable mention.

But the Wazzu was never far from his thoughts. "What if I went to Washington State," he daydreamed, "and all of a sudden something happened and I was a starter as a true freshman? How would I deal with it?"

WSU coach Mike Price wanted Drew to play for him.

The Cougars had two good quarterbacks—a fifth-year senior named Brad Gossen and a talented sophomore named Aaron Garcia—so Drew's dream was crazy. Or was it?

Drew moved to Pullman and rented an apartment near campus with Robbie Tobeck, the team's center. Drew decided to major in English. In football, Drew took jersey number 11—the number that his high school workout pal Andy Jamison had worn. Drew knew that he would never have gotten a scholarship without Jamison. At Texas Christian University for the season opener, Drew warmed up with his team's two veteran quarterbacks at one end of the field. Coach Price was chatting near midfield with TCU coach Jim Wacker. "Who the heck is number 11?" Wacker suddenly asked. "He's not going to play, is he?" Drew did not play in that game or in the next one. Then Coach Price put him in for the last few moments of a game against Brigham Young University, and he completed two of three passes. The next two games, he sat.

Drew wore No. 11 in honor of his high school friend.

Then against the University of Southern California at the Los Angeles Memorial Coliseum, Drew was sent in to play the second half. "I ran onto the field and looked around the Coliseum, and it was just like a dream," he said. "There was this big replay screen at one end that showed me running down the field, and when I looked up and saw it, I realized I wasn't dreaming." He completed 6 of 12 passes for 145 yards and a touchdown. At practice the next week, Coach Price said Drew would start the Oregon State game. That's when the trouble started.

As a freshman, Drew wasn't expected to start.

"When the announcement was made, the team sort of divided itself," said Drew. Some players felt that, as a senior, Gossen deserved to start. Others wanted Garcia, who had replaced Gossen the previous year and led the conference in passing. Still others thought Drew was the best of the three. "It was ugly," Drew said. "There were three separate cliques on the team, and the ones that weren't for me wouldn't talk to me.

Drew's strong arm and smart play won over his teammates.

Running backs and receivers I was throwing to would come back to the huddle and never say a word to me. It was the toughest thing I had to deal with in my life. I think I handled it as best I could. I just kept my mouth shut and played."

In Drew's first start, he led the Cougars to 46 first-half points in a 55–24 win. On one play, Gossen and Garcia realized why they would never again play for Washington State. Running under pressure to the sideline, Drew stopped and gunned the ball across his body 40 yards to tight end Butch Williams who was near the opposite side of the field. "I could do that," Gossen muttered to the coach. "I could do that," Garcia said.

Then Gossen and Garcia looked at each other and broke out laughing. They knew they could not have done that, and they realized just how good Drew was.

As a sophomore, Drew emerged as a star. Coach Price had given him the playbook and told him to find a way to win. On the field, Drew called so many passes both teams got dizzy. "It's exciting," he said of playing in Pullman. "On Saturdays, football is the whole show. Everything shuts down because of the game." Drew's family joined in the fun. They had moved to Yakima where Mac coached and Adam played quarterback. Friday nights after the high school game, they would leave for Pullman. Mac would drive their '54 Chevy four hours east while Barbara and Adam slept in the back.

Drew torched opponents for 2,647 yards, leading the conference in total offense. He threw five touchdowns against Oregon State and three more against Arizona and Washington. "This is my 11th year in the league, and I've seen a lot of quarterbacks," said Oregon State defensive coach Osla Lewis. "He is the best guy since [John] Elway, as far as a pure **drop-back passer.**" But the Cougars struggled on the offensive line. They averaged just 3 yards rushing, and Drew was sacked 56 times.

As Drew's junior season approached, football experts began talking about his chances to become a professional. Some thought he would be a top pick if he left college early. "Bledsoe is number 1," said one expert. "There's a big difference between him and everyone else. I've never been this sure about a number 1 pick."

Drew and his parents downplayed the fuss. "I'd say I'm a little surprised," said Drew. "I personally feel I didn't have that great a year last year." Barbara said her son should not look that far ahead. "He's 20 years old," she said. "He just needs to be a 20-year-old, play ball, and go to school." Someday, they thought, Drew might be lucky enough to sign an NFL contract. In the meantime, he drove around the Wazzu campus in his beat-up Ford Granada, with its dangling muffler and one hubcap.

As a junior, Drew broke nearly every school passing record. After throwing for 413 yards and three touchdowns against Montana in the season opener and then directing his team to late game-winning scores against Arizona and Fresno State in the next two games, Drew admitted, "I've improved a lot." He finished the season with 3,246 yards and 20 touchdowns and was named the Pac-10 Conference's Most Valuable Player. He capped it off with a sparkling 476-yard performance and a victory in the Copper Bowl.

Despite Drew's excellent performance, he wasn't a big shot at his school. "He's not viewed as a celebrity on campus," his father said. "Most of his professors don't even know he plays football."

As a junior, Drew led WSU to a victory in the Copper Bowl.

Near the end of his junior year, Drew agreed to go on a blind date to play tennis. His date, a student named Maura Healy, beat him in singles. He challenged her to another match, and before long they were dating regularly.

On January 4, 1993, Drew announced at a press conference that he would skip his senior year and enter the NFL draft. "I always wanted to play on Sundays on television," he told reporters as cameras clicked and whirred. "Playing in the NFL is a dream come true. But still, it's funny to think that someone would pay me to play."

The New England Patriots looked to their rookie quarterback
to lead them to success in the 1993 season.

4

A New Challenge

The New England Patriots were losers. They rarely won even half their games. One year (1986) they made it to the Super Bowl, only to lose the game by the most points in NFL history (36). In 1992, the Patriots had finished with the worst record in the league, so they held the first choice in the spring draft. They thought they would pick Drew.

The Patriots wanted to meet Drew first. So he and his agent, Leigh Steinberg, flew to Boston, Massachusetts, to meet head coach Bill Parcells and his staff. Parcells had won two Super Bowls while coaching the New York Giants. He had a reputation as a loud-mouthed disciplinarian with a large ego and a sharp needle for his players. After spending the day with Coach Parcells, Drew told reporters, "He's a lot more real than I thought he would be. He didn't tell me how great I was. He just said I was a good prospect." Drew was being polite. At the meeting, Parcells had told Drew that there were better quarterbacks to draft. Steinberg described the coach that day as "arrogant, challenging, insulting."

The Patriots drafted Drew anyway. Drew asked for jersey number 11 again, in honor of his friend, Andy Jamison. Then he signed a six-year contract for $14.5 million. He was so stunned at his sudden wealth that he had 15-year-old Adam call his bank to listen to the computer rattle off how much money there was in his account. Drew moved into an apartment in the same building as Patriots players Eugene Chung and Todd Rucci. Then he sat down with the Patriots' thick playbook and began to study.

Four quarterbacks had started games for the Patriots the year before. None was very good. Coaches don't like to play rookie quarterbacks, but the team was desperate. Drew knew he had a chance to start. In the team's preseason opener against the San Diego Chargers, he completed his first professional pass, a 9-yarder. "That made me feel good," said Drew. Later in the game, he threw a touchdown to Troy Brown. Afterward, Drew said the biggest difference from college to the pros is the speed of the game. "Everything is so intense," he said. "Everything happens so much faster."

By the end of preseason, Drew was the team's starter, and fans were sure he would rescue the team.

But Drew knew he was just a rookie, trying to find his way in the league. "I'm happy with my progress," he said, "but I know I have a long way to go. There are still times when I'm kind of unsure what's happening."

New England lost its first four games, won one, then lost seven more. Drew led plenty of nice drives, but he could not do it all himself. "People have to remember I'm the foundation. I'm not everything," he said. "All the coaches are so uptight. I'm aware that I'm young. I'm only two and a half years from being a teenager." Drew took losing hard. After a 45–7 loss to the New York Jets, he said, "It was just a humiliating feeling walking off the field."

Practice wasn't any easier. Coach Parcells made Drew fetch cups of Gatorade for him. The coach stood behind his quarterback at the line of scrimmage and yelled words like "You stink!" at him.

"Sometimes," Drew admitted, "I just want to turn around and scream 'Shut up!'" Parcells said he was just trying to distract Drew, but others said the coach was jealous that his quarterback got so much media attention. When Drew led the Patriots to four straight wins to close the season—including a 33–27 overtime victory against the Miami Dolphins—his popularity soared. Children throughout the Boston area suddenly were wearing number 11 jerseys. Drew was hounded for autographs everywhere he went. Fans even came knocking on his door.

Optimism flowed at training camp in the summer of 1994. Linebacker Willie McGinest said, "Dallas has Troy Aikman at quarterback. We've got Drew Bledsoe. We fully expect to be as good." Fans around the team's practice facility in Smithfield, Rhode Island, screamed Drew's name. Reporters gathered around him for interviews. Coach Parcells told Drew one day, "Just remember one thing: I don't want a celebrity quarterback on my team. I hate celebrity quarterbacks. You understand?"

The Patriots lost their first two games, even though Drew led them to five touchdowns each time. They won their next three, but lost their next four. In the next game, the Patriots were trailing the Minnesota Vikings 20–3 at halftime. Drew rallied his team to tie the score. In the overtime, Drew lobbed a 14-yarder to fullback Kevin Turner in the corner of the end zone to win the game. In the locker room, Coach Parcells started to cry. "You've given me hope," he said to Drew. "That was valiant." The Patriots won their last seven games to make the playoffs for the first time in eight years.

New England was back in the playoffs, but not for long. The Patriots lost in Cleveland to the Browns, 20–13. Drew threw three interceptions. He had one final chance to tie the game, after the Patriots kicked a field goal and then recovered an **onside kick** at their 36-yard line with a minute and a half to play.

Drew's poise under pressure helped the Patriots win.

But after quickly moving the ball to midfield, he threw four straight **incompletions.** "They came in here thinking Bledsoe could beat us," said Browns defensive end Rob Burnett. "He couldn't." It was a painful ending to a storybook season for Drew. He had completed 400 passes for a team-record 4,555 yards and 25 touchdowns. And, he was the youngest quarterback to ever play in the Pro Bowl.

Midway through the season, Drew bought a five-bedroom house in a quiet neighborhood in Bridgewater, Massachusetts. He filled it with computers and laser disc players. "I'm in the generation that grew up with Atari and Nintendo," he said. "By the time I was in sixth grade, we had computers in our classrooms. I have no fear of these things." After the season, he flew to Walla Walla to sign autographs and to give $110,000 to the YMCA for new weight machines. While he was there, he gave his Patriots jersey to Andy Jamison. Drew said, "I'm proud to wear your number in the NFL, Andy."

Drew enjoyed being generous, and the new Patriots owner, Robert Kraft, made it easy for him. Kraft signed Drew to a seven-year deal for $42 million. Drew was the highest-paid player in the history of the game. "We believe we have the best young player in the NFL," said Kraft, "and I wanted to sign him as soon as I took over the team." Drew could not believe how much money he was making.

Drew hugs his mom at the Walla Walla YMCA.

"Two and a half years ago, I was driving a 1977 Ford Granada," he said, "and when they gave me $100,000 for a trading card thing [so they could use his picture], it was unfathomable. Then after that, the money was just all numbers."

The Patriots avenged their 1994 playoff loss to the Browns by beating them in the 1995 season opener. But their fortunes for the year changed in the third game at San Francisco. Drew dropped back to pass when 49ers linebacker Ken Norton Jr. charged in on a blitz and hit him. Drew was taken to the locker room, where his left shoulder was taped together. He played in the second half, but he winced when he threw. After the game, the doctors said that his shoulder was separated. He missed the next game and played the next several in pain.

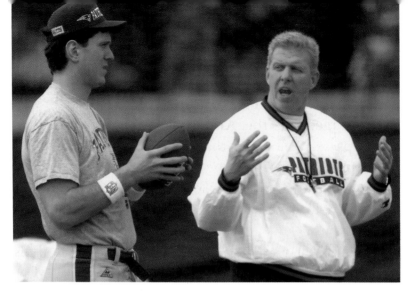
Drew and Coach Parcells didn't get along very well.

Coach Parcells continued to scream at his quarterback on the sideline even as the season faded away. Drew said, "I don't believe he's going to make me play any better by yelling at me the way he does." Drew's family agreed. "I don't like it," said Barbara. "That's not going to help Drew perform better." When Parcells was told of her remark, he snapped "Tell her not to watch the games." New England missed the playoffs.

Drew's life off the field was much better. He and Maura Healy had decided to get married. They told their relatives and friends at a party in Washington. Drew said, "I want my best friend to be my best man." He walked up to his brother, Adam, and said, "Well, kid, will you do it?" Drew and Maura were married in her hometown of Portland, Oregon, in May 1996.

Then came that glorious Super Bowl season. The Patriots raced to the AFC Eastern Division title as Drew passed for more than 4,000 yards for the second time. The night before the divisional game against the Pittsburgh Steelers, his father told him, as he does before every game, "Good luck. Throw it to our guys."

In the fog at Foxboro Stadium, Drew completed his first seven passes for 123 yards and a touchdown. The Patriots jumped out to a 21–0 halftime lead. They cruised to a 28–3 win, the first home playoff victory in team history. In the AFC title game against the Jacksonville Jaguars a week later at Foxboro, Drew endured subfreezing conditions to guide his team to a 20–6 victory and a trip to the 1997 Super Bowl.

In the days leading up to the Super Bowl, there was talk that this would be Coach Parcells' last game with the Patriots. He was rumored to be headed to coach the New York Jets. Reporters knew how the coach had treated Drew and they asked him what he thought about the rumors.

"Whether Bill is here or not, this team is going to be successful," Drew said. "Look, Bill told me from the beginning, 'I'm not going to be your coach forever.' Sometimes, that's a pretty enticing proposition." The Patriots lost the Super Bowl, and then they lost their coach. Drew was disappointed with one loss, but not the other.

Drew and Coach Carroll took the Patriots to the AFC East title game in Carroll's first year as coach.

5

Patriot Games

The new season was like a breath of fresh air for Drew. Pete Carroll had become head coach of the Patriots, and Drew felt happy and free. "I'm glad that I played for Bill. I'm a tougher player for it," Drew said. "But I really enjoy playing for Pete. He's positive. He's upbeat. He treats you with respect and dignity, rather than berating you."

When Parcells showed up at Foxboro Stadium with his Jets for an early-season game, Drew rallied his team to a 27–24 overtime victory against his old coach. From there, the Patriots rolled to the AFC East title once again, but this time they lost to the Steelers, 7–6, in the first round of the 1998 playoffs. The bitter one-point loss left Drew more determined than ever.

Drew expects more from himself than just reaching the playoffs each season. "It's made me hungry after taking part in the Super Bowl and losing, to get back there and win it," he said. "My expectations are pretty high and I have never met them. If you're completely satisfied with what you've accomplished, you'll never get better."

Drew finds time to enjoy himself off the football field as well. He likes running around the park with his golden retriever, Billie, and black Lab, Jake. He also loves racing across the lake on his jet-ski, or going on an upside-down flight with the Navy's Blue Angels.

Drew spends a lot of time doing things to make others happy. He is always the last player off the practice field because he stops to sign 200 or 300 autographs. He visits elementary schools and performs the only magic trick he says he knows—handing kids envelopes and making $20 appear in each one. He enjoys making such appearances as long as he is seen as just a football player and nothing more. He knows people can get carried away.

Once when he appeared to speak at a university, the university's president introduced him by saying, "If this guy stays on track, he's going to personally turn America's youth around."

"I become an NFL quarterback and all of a sudden people think I'm an authority on everything," Drew says, laughing. "I go home and get treated the same way as I always have. Having to take out the trash and do the dishes, that helps a bunch."

Drew gives Patriots fans a big thumbs-up during a
pre-Super Bowl pep rally.

As long as Drew plays football—pitching and handing off to his backs, flicking passes down the middle, occasionally airing out a long one, and grinning as he goes—he will stay humble, no matter how many Super Bowls he wins or how much money he earns. "It's twisted making so much to play football," he says. "My parents are both schoolteachers and there's no way I can sit here and tell you they are not both benefiting society more by what they do than what I do. My first year in football—my father and I figured this out—I was making 200 years' worth of my dad's salary. It's unfathomable. It's twisted and it's kind of a reflection on our society of what we view as important.

"Football is a big part of my life but it's not in the three or four most important things in life. It's football.

Drew hugs one of his teammates after a Patriots' score.

Drew's parents, Barbara and Mac, love taking care of their grandson, Drew's son, Stu McQueen Bledsoe.

It just seems ludicrous to me that someone would say football should be the number one priority in your life. My parents were always good at reminding me what was really important." Or, as his father says, "Home is where you go even if you don't throw touchdowns."

What is important to Drew is his wife, Maura, their son, Stu McQueen Bledsoe—who was born in November 1997—Drew's brother, their grandparents and parents, and Drew's friends. "It doesn't matter to my parents and family whether or not I play football," Drew says. "They're still my parents and family, and all this other stuff is just fun and adventure."

Career Highlights

College Statistics

Year	Team	Attempts	Comps	Yards	Pct	TDs	INTs
1990	Washington State	189	92	1,386	48.7	9	4
1991	Washington State	358	199	2,741	55.6	17	15
1992	Washington State	432	241	3,246	55.8	20	15

Pro Statistics

Year	Team	Attempts	Comps	Yards	Pct	TDs	INTs
1993	New England	429	214	2,494	49.9	15	15
1994	New England	691	400	4,555	57.9	25	27
1995	New England	636	323	3,507	50.8	13	16
1996	New England	623	373	4,086	59.9	27	15
1997	New England	522	314	3,706	60.2	28	15

Glossary

blitz: Sending defenders directly at the quarterback.

conversion: Scoring the extra points after a touchdown, either with a pass, a run, or a kick.

defensive formations: Positioning of defensive players to stop the opponent from running or passing.

down: An attempt to advance the football. A team gets four downs to advance 10 yards or score.

drop-back passer: A quarterback who moves straight back about five yards behind the blockers and stops before throwing a pass.

incompletions: Passes that are not caught.

onside kick: A short kick on a kickoff that the kicking team hopes to recover near midfield. The kick must go at least 10 yards.

play-fakes: Plays that are designed to fool an opponent. For example, a quarterback might pretend to hand the ball to a running back but then throw the ball to a receiver.

screen pass: A pass to a receiver who is at or behind the line of scrimmage and who is protected by blockers.

turnovers: Losing the ball, either because of a fumble or an interception.

Sources

Information for this book was obtained from the author's interviews with Barbara Bledsoe, Mac Bledsoe, Gary Mires, and the following sources: Bill Brink (*New York Times*, 27 January 1997); Nick Carfado (*Boston Globe*, 18 July 1997); Tony Cooper (*San Francisco Chronicle*, 12 November 1992); Michael Gee (*Boston Herald*, 27 January 1997); Dale Grummert (*Lewiston Morning Tribune*, 15 November 1991); Scott Kauffman (*USA TODAY*, 13 October 1992); Peter King (*Sports Illustrated*, 6 December 1993, 4 September 1995); J. M. Lawrence (*Boston Herald*, 22 January 1997); Frank Litsky (*New York Times*, 31 August 1993); Michael Madden (*Boston Globe*, 9 August 1993, 27 July 1995); Michael Martinez (*New York Times*, 28 October 1992); Austin Murphy (*Sports Illustrated*, 27 January 1997); New England Patriots 1997 Media Guide; Bruce Newman (*Sports Illustrated*, 6 April 1993); Charles P. Pierce (*Boston Magazine*, October 1993); Charles P. Pierce (*Boston Globe*, 18 September 1994); Steve Rivera (*Tucson Citizen*, 8 September 1992); Timothy W. Smith (*New York Times*, 2 January 1995); Mark Starr (*Newsweek*, 28 August 1995); Samantha Stevenson (*New York Times*, 15 April 1993); Rick Telander (*Sports Illustrated*, 7 November 1994); Washington State University 1992 Media Guide; Bud Withers (*Seattle Post-Intelligencer*, 26 August 1992, 3 September 1992).

Index

Write to Drew

You can send mail to Drew at the address on the right. If you write a letter, don't get your hopes up too high. Drew and other athletes get lots of letters every day, and they aren't always able to answer them all.

Drew Bledsoe
c/o New England Patriots
60 Washington Street
Foxboro, MA 02035

Acknowledgments

Photographs reproduced with permission of: © SportsChrome East/West, Rich Kane, pp. 1, 6, 49, 54, 58; © SportsChrome East/West, Rob Tringali Jr., pp. 2, 10; © Mickey Pfleger/Endzone, pp. 9, 13; Reuters/Adrees Latiff/Archive Photos, p. 14; © Bruce Gordon/Endzone, p. 16; Agence France Presse/Corbis-Bettmann, p. 17; Drew Bledsoe Foundation, pp. 18, 20, 21, 23, 24, 25, 27, 28, 51, 59; Seth Poppel Yearbook Archives, pp. 31, 33, 34; Seattle Spokesman-Review, pp. 36, 37, 43; Washington State University, Sports Information, pp. 38, 39, 40; © ALLSPORT USA/Rick Stewart, p. 44; Reuters/Gary Hershorn/Archive Photos, p. 52; Reuters/Brian Snyder/Archive Photos, p. 57.

Front cover photograph by © SportsChrome East/West, Rich Kane. Back cover photograph from the Drew Bledsoe Foundation.

Artwork by Lejla Fazlic Omerovic.

About the Author

Jeff Savage is the author of more than 30 sports books for young readers, including Lerner's *Tiger Woods*, *Grant Hill*, and *Eric Lindros*. A freelance writer, Jeff lives with his family in California.

64